HUMMINGBIRD WISDOM FOR KIDS
Enlightening Hearts of All Ages

Written and Illustrated by
Rosemary Watson, Ph.D.

Copyright © 2018 by Rosemary Watson, Ph.D. 770071
Library of Congress Control Number: Pending

All rights reserved. No part of this book may be reproduced
or transmitted in any form or by any means, electronic or
mechanical, including photocopying, recording, or by any
information storage and retrieval system, without permission in
writing from the copyright owner.

This is a work of fiction. Names, characters, places and incidents
either are the product of the author's imagination or are used
fictitiously, and any resemblance to any actual persons, living or
dead, events, or locales is entirely coincidental.

ISBN:
Hardcover: 978-1-962342-96-4
Paperback: 978-1-962342-97-1

HUMMINGBIRD WISDOM FOR KIDS

Enlightening Hearts of All Ages

Written and Illustrated by
Rosemary Watson, Ph.D.

Contents

CHAPTER 1 – JEWEL DUSTER 11

CHAPTER 2 – ENERGY VIBRATION: HIGH OR LOW? 17

CHAPTER 3 – BABY BLUEY FINDS HIS PURPOSE 26

CHAPTER 4 – MOTHER NATURE'S RHYTHMS..33

CHAPTER 5 – A CREEPY-CRAWLER TRANSFORMS 39

CHAPTER 6 – THE BLIND SPIDER SEES 45

CHAPTER 7 – I FOUND MY MATE! 51

CHAPTER 8 – TRANSFORMING TROUBLE INTO PEACE 58

CHAPTER 9 – THE GARDEN OF ENCHANTMENTS 63

CHAPTER 10 – ENLIGHTENED BABY HUMMERS 70

About the Author 77

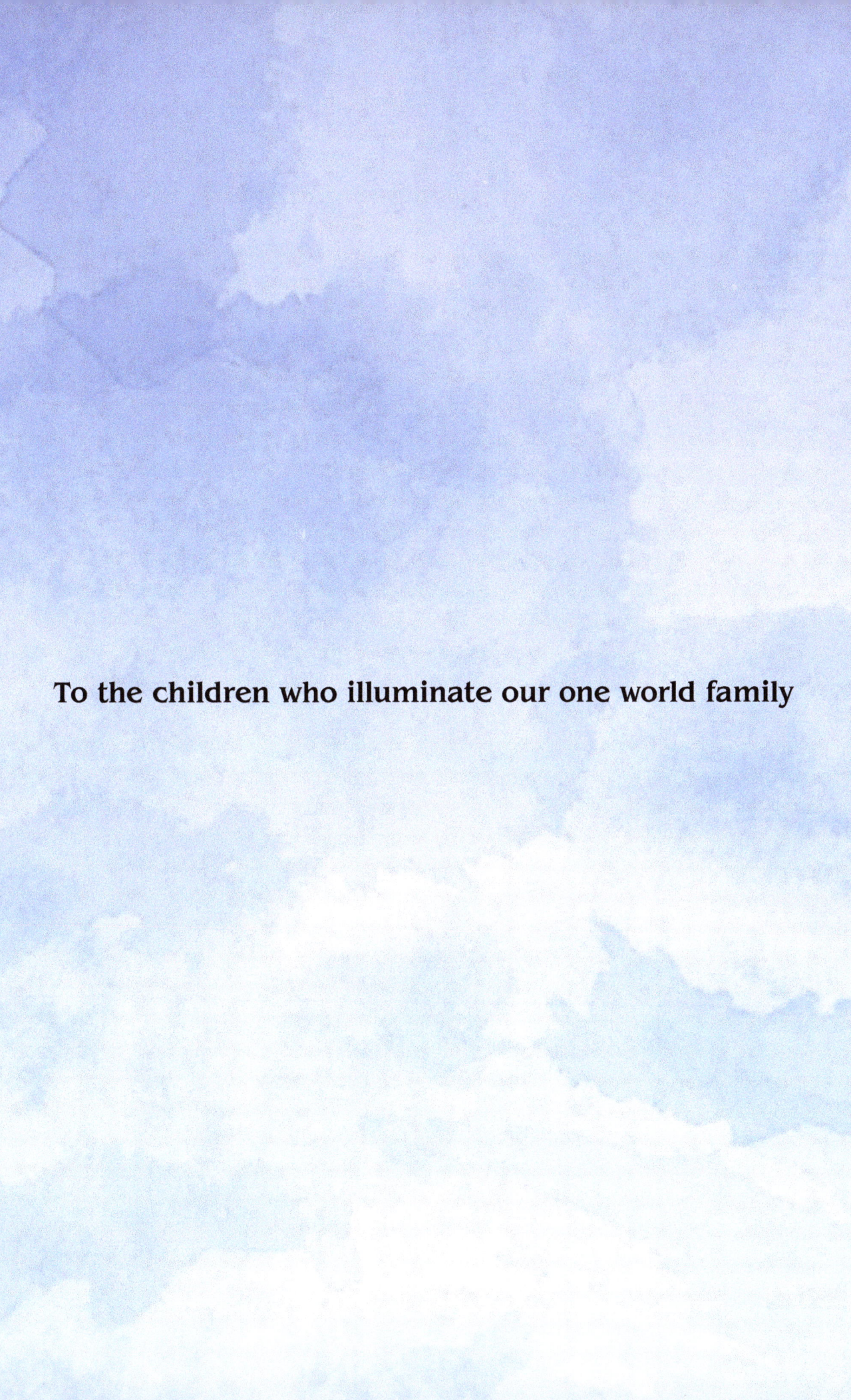

To the children who illuminate our one world family

Introduction

Nature can be our greatest teacher if we open up to creativity and intelligence, and playing with children's imagination. As children face daily conflicts, opportunities arise for learning growth, and enrichment. When they are stuck in an emotional dump, there are many skills and tools available to turn things around to find preferred outcomes. As Mother Nature's rhythms play and flow—sometimes chaotically bringing in fire, floods, or earthquakes—so, too, do humans encounter disturbing changes in their mental and emotional rhythms. And as in nature, where there is calm after the storm, we, too, can turn to calm, inner stillness to find the clearest means to rise above it all.

In *Hummingbird Wisdom for Kids*, a family of wise hummingbirds establishes a beautiful Garden of Great Love. In tune with Mother Nature, they are guided by their inner vision of loving kindness. From a very young age, they are taught to transform conflicts into peace, danger into safety, and anger into love.

The following are some of the hummingbird seeds of wisdom planted in each chapter:

Within a tiny seed is the power to create a giant tree.

All rhythms come from one source.

Metamorphosis is the sweetest freedom.

Turning trouble into peace can brighten your life.

Even tiny hearts can feel love that is as big as the ocean.

<u>Learning Instruction for Young Readers</u>

Some parts of this story are factual, and some are fantasy. Can you guess which is which? Google hummingbird facts and find out. Test your knowledge and enliven your wisdom. Life's adventure is greatly enhanced when one's potential is unfolded and inner treasures are revealed.

Hummingbird Wisdom for Kids
Tales that will enlighten the hearts of kids of all ages.

ABOUT THE BOOK

Four generations of hummingbirds share their tales of wisdom, joy and love for nature. These hummingbird families live by universal truths to maintain peace and loving kindness. With their daily habits of settling in Torpor, a regenerating inner stillness, they connect with Mother Nature's rhythms to masterfully pollinate and beautify the gardens of great love.

The main character, a female hummer, rescues a trapped male hummer from a poisonous spider. Later, he performs an alluring dance that convinces her that he's the one. As the time comes for their offspring, they fight to keep the peace among strange, dangerous animals lurking in the garden. A visit to grandma proves to illuminate the young hummers, as their visions open to new possibilities for rising above destructive forces.

Can the hummingbirds be victorious against destructive forces that are hundreds of times larger than them? Their only weapon used to preserve their garden of great love is peace and loving kindness. The tiny hummers know how to transmute matter with their supernatural abilities such as the jewel duster, imagination projector and the colorful healing laser beams. Each generation magnifies these natural superpowers as their energy vibrations rise higher and higher.

In each tale, an important lesson is given. Planted throughout the ten chapters of this story book are charming seeds of hummingbird wisdom that will warm your heart. A hummingbird teaches a bluebird to avoid danger by using the power of imagination. An energy vibration chart is mentally transmitted from father to daughter showing how negative destructive energy can be transformed into positive constructive energy. A creepy crawler explains how she changed herself into a beautiful being of the air.

Throughout the story book, unfriendly garden creatures are transformed from unhappy hostile beings to caring, happier beings as they awaken to the one source that hums beneath all of life. As more and more garden creatures raise their energy vibrations they join forces in the rhythms of flow and play, and build more beautiful gardens. They learn to be in perfect stillness, so they can respond wisely to any situation.

CHAPTER 1 – JEWEL DUSTER

It was a perfect spring day in sunny California. New life was popping up everywhere. The orange tree had white flowers that filled the air with fragrance. Cute little baby birds were hatching and bobbing up and down in nests. Playful baby bunnies were hopping all around. And high up in a tree sat a tiny gray hummingbird. She was not as alluring as the male hummingbirds. They would flicker their wings and catch iridescent colors in the sunlight. But she had something more beautiful than just pretty feathers. This little hummingbird had iridescent wisdom. If garden friends were in danger, in a flash she found a way to rescue them. She knew how to turn trouble into peace.

The little bird knew she was very lucky because she came from a family rich in hummingbird wisdom. These riches couldn't be lost or stolen. With wisdom, a dry, ugly garden will turn into a magical place filled with brilliant flowers, elegant trees, and happy playful creatures. With joy she would do whatever was needed to keep the garden blossoming. That's why her family named her Joyful Eve.

When Joyful was a baby, her mama, Karuna, taught her to have a big heart even though she had a tiny body. Mama Karuna had soft peachy-pink feathers and was known for being a wiz with rhythms. She used a flowing rhythm to glide in and out of the winds, dancing with poetic tempo. When it was time to build a nest, she used mechanical rhythms to make it sturdy, as hummingbirds often come back to their nest to lay more eggs. Karuna knew how to stay safe even in Mother Nature's chaotic rhythms, such as wild fires, earthquakes, and crazy storms. And to recharge her energy and sharpen her skills she would use the stillness rhythm in sleep and in Torpor.

Karuna taught Joyful that Mother Nature was the master teacher, so Joyful grew up learning from nature. She watched the baby squirrels giggling and flipping their tails. From their playful rhythm, she learned how important it is to be creative and have fun. She studied the army of ants carrying leaves as they marched to mechanical rhythms: one, two, three, and four. From them she learned to stay focused to accomplish goals. She watched the mama koi fish swim with her babies in flowing rhythms. From the koi, she learned how to go with the flow of life.

In playful rhythms, Joyful zoomed and zipped from flower to flower, sipping and slurping the sweetest nectar.

She chimed with a buzzing hum, "Flowers grow in light, love grows in light, and my heart has wings of light."

In this garden, there lived a kind couple named Janet and Jack who hung a bird feeder filled with nectar on their balcony. Many hummingbirds would zoom over to drink, but then they would chase and attack one another. Joyful thought, *there is enough for all if only they would share.*

One day, while watching the hummingbirds argue from high up in a tree, Joyful saw a mischievous raccoon peeking through a bush. She wondered, *is he planning to do something cruel?* More than anything Joyful wanted the Garden of Great Love to be a place where everyone was loving and kind.

Just then, Joyful heard her friend Lupee the koi fish crying for help. In a flash she flew to the pond. Lupee and her five babies looked scared and jittery.

Lupee splattered water as she burbled to Joyful, "Last night, Rascal Lee, that mad bandit raccoon, jumped into our pond. He was out of control, chasing us for hours and tearing up all the plants. We scattered, fearing for our lives, and hid beneath the rocks. He finally gave up and left. Next time, I'm not sure if we can escape his razor-sharp teeth. Can you do something to stop him?"

Joyful looked at Lupee's babies and chirped with compassion, "Of course I will help. Tonight, when the stars come out, I'll be ready!"

That night, the garden was quiet, and the stars were twinkling in a dark-blue sky. Rascal Lee climbed over the fence and slinked into the pond.

Joyful heard Lupee blurt to her babies, "The bandito is here! Swim fast! Quick, hide! Don't let him get you!"

They all scurried and jumped like firecrackers in the pond.

One baby koi moaned, "Help me, Mama!"

Another baby puffed and blubbered, "He almost got me!"

Another one screeched, "Help me—he's got me in his claws. It hurts! I'm so scared."

Rascal Lee's whiskers stiffened. He held the baby koi in his sharp claws and grunted, "Yum, I got a flappin' good meal."

Lupee slapped him with her fins. She sucked in prickly leaves and spit them at him, then yelled, "Stop, stop, please let him go!"

Rascal Lee was about to eat the baby koi when Joyful zoomed by him with lightning speed. She thought, *what can I do? He's so much bigger than me!* Then she remembered her Jewel Duster, which brightens the light in her heart and vibrates energy higher and faster. It could give her the power to change what Rascal Lee was thinking. In a flash she hovered over him, spraying him with sparkling jewel dust. It dazzled him with rainbow colors that disappeared into his body. Then the changes started to happen!

Rascal Lee became very quiet. His body buzzed with new energy and color. The baby koi slipped out of his paw and swam for shelter. With a grin on his face, he whispered, "What am I doing? I don't want to hurt this baby fish."

"Look how his mood is changing!" chirped Joyful to Lupee. "Did you see when Rascal Lee was about to hurt your baby, his energy colors changed from dull to bright? Now he is smiling instead of snarling."

"Yes. It's remarkable!" bubbled Lupee. "But what happened? I don't understand."

"When you are happy, your energy vibrates higher and you just don't want to hurt anybody. So, that's what happened to him," Joyful whistled gleefully. "As the jewel dust entered his body, the dark energy clouds of bad thoughts and feelings just disappeared. Rascal Lee came back to his kind nature."

Meanwhile, Rascal Lee slowly rolled on his back and floated in the pond with a goofy smile on his face. The moon was smiling at him, and he was smiling back.

"Wow, I feel phenomenal!" chuckled Rascal Lee. "Just awhile ago, I would have attacked anything in sight. And now I say, 'No way!' And who turned the lights on? Everything around me looks so much brighter and beautiful." Then he sat on the pond's edge. As he scratched his head, he thought, *But I'm still hungry.*

Just then an apple fell to the ground and rolled right next to him. He picked it up, sniffed it, and devoured it. Several more apples fell, and he quickly gobbled them up, too. With his belly full, he stretched out his slinky, hairy legs and fell asleep on the soft grass.

Lupee jumped out of the water and did a triple pirouette in the air. With happy stars around her eyes, she bubbled kisses and said, "Thank you, Joyful, for saving my babies." They all flapped their fins and swam around gracefully knowing Rascal Lee was now an ally.

Joyful was thrilled. She thought, *Yay, they are safe! Even Rascal Lee. When you find loving kindness inside you, you can't be mean to others.*

And then it happened: the gray feathers around Joyful's crown changed to yellow, amber, and honey—just like Lupee's shimmering scales.

Hummingbird Wisdom: A sprinkle of jewel dust can prevent a lifetime of sadness.

CHAPTER 2 – ENERGY VIBRATION: HIGH OR LOW?

On top of the hill, above the garden, grew a royal jacaranda tree with a large trunk and lots of strong, curly branches. Joyful was born in this tree. Every year in June, she watched purple flowers unfold their petals from small buds to hundreds of blossoms. This is one of Mother Nature's celestial gifts.

In a nest tucked in the tree, she began to learn hummingbird wisdom. Her parents taught her to listen and watch for rhythms such as rustling winds and jangling leaves to forecast the weather. Everything gave her special messages by how its energy vibrated. This she learned from her father, Kindheart. He had velvety-blue feathers with white tips and amber eyes. He was an expert in energy and vibration.

Father Kindheart knew when energy was vibrating very low, because it would be dense, heavy, and slow, with dark and dull tones. He knew when energy was vibrating high, because it would be clear, light, and fast with light and bright colors. He told Joyful that the wisest ones always vibrate ultra-high and radiate the brightest light. When you have superintelligence, you find more opportunities and solutions than conflicts and problems. With fewer worries, there is more fun and joy. What she remembered best was that special day when he willed the sunset to form the shape of a heart.

Joyful recalled one time when a hungry cat was going after cute baby squirrels tucked away in a tree trunk. Father Kindheart dive-bombed the cat, leading it to a bowl of food left in front of a nearby house. He said to mother squirrel, Fluffy Tail, "If you want to make it seem like you are bigger than the cat, then make loud scary sounds and stiffen your tail—lift it high and flick warnings at him or send big waves of love to him. It might just turn him around to be a friend and not a foe." Fluffy Tail chittered that she liked the idea of practicing kindness and thanked him. Later, she left him special seeds in his family's nest.

As Joyful was thinking of Fluffy Tail, she heard a rustling of leaves above her. She looked up, and there was Kindheart perched above her. Happily she flew up next to him. "How wonderful to see you!" she trilled in a high-pitched chirp.

Father Kindheart announced, "I've come to remind you how baby birds are created."

Joyful giggled. "Are you going to tell me the joke about the yoke?"

"Yes, you are still a silly hummer." Father Kindheart laughed. "Soon you will have your own eggs that will be baby hummers. Can you tell me how a chick develops inside the egg?"

"I do know how eggs become chicks. Inside the egg is a powerful electrical energy that is superintelligent and creative. It's the one source from where all things are create," sang Joyful.

"Good! And do you understand this energy source and how all creation comes from it?" twittered Father Kindheart.

"Yes, you use your thoughts, feelings and beliefs to manifest what you want." Joyful tweeted happily.

He responded, "Did you know that the ability to get energy whenever you want is an awesome gift from nature?"

"Yes, you mean like practicing Torpor to get supercharged? Torpor sometimes feels like a peaceful hovering inside of me?"

"Very good. This is the essence of hummingbird wisdom. With the gift of Torpor we become re-energized and empowered whenever we want. It is connecting with the source energy like electrical energy that keeps things alive, growing and expanding. Consider the intelligence in the sun, moon, and stars as they move with order in a constant direction. It is the same energy source inside the seed that has the intelligence to sprout then spiral up toward the light to become beautiful plants and trees. This is the same energy source in you and me. In the stillness of Torpor, we connect with that energy source, which grows and expands, unfolding more intelligence and wisdom."

Joyful said, "Got it! Every animal, mammal, bird, insect, and plant has its very own special gift that guides it with intelligence to do all the amazing things they do. I guess that's it, in an eggshell."

Father Kindheart laughed. "Yep, that's it. When we go for the highest energy level, everything you want is given to you. And you are an exquisite gift in the Garden of Great Love. You are my perfect little hummer."

My father must be very well connected with the great energy source, because he is brilliant, thought Joyful.

Father Kindheart continued. "I am sending you two pictures, one made of positive energy and the other made of negative energy.

"Do you see now that all living things have their own special vibration? chirped Kindheart. And do you understand how they are connected to one source that lives in all things? Mother Nature always helps those who are vibrating with ultra-high energy to make their dreams come true."

"Yes!" she squealed with excitement as she hovered in the air. "I love being of part of the positive high energy that make everything bright and beautiful. Yes, I love how the flowers vibrate superhigh energy, smell so great, and give me sweet nectar."

They smiled and twinkled with love for each other as they closed their eyes and went into the quiet stillness of Torpor. Together they listened to the cosmic hum and knew it as the engine that kept creation going.

As they opened their eyes, father Kindheart said, "I am sending you an energy vibrations chart. It will give you a clearer picture of how low energy and high energy work in the world. Study it and you'll will become a master navigator."

ENERGY VIBRATION CHART

ENERGY VIBRATION LEVEL	MENTAL ACTIVITY	EMOTIONAL OUTCOME
Very High to Ultra-High **Positive energy rules**	**I think I am....** **I am ever blossoming**	**I feel....** **Emotional Intelligence Excels**
100	Loved by nature, it's perfect	Pure love, bliss
95	Enthusiastic, goodwill to all	Serene, joyful
90	Insightful, beautiful imagination	Harmonious, intuitive
85	Knowledgeable, giving	Friendly, trusting
80	Inspirational, motivated	Relaxed, self-comforting
75	Thoughtful, adaptable	Thoughtful and adaptable
70	Fair-minded, self-encouraging	Fair-minded and encouraging
Low to High **Energy transforms from negative to positive**	**I think I am....** **I am responsible for learning and growing wiser.**	**I feel....** **I can identify each emotion, understand and express it.**
65	Expanding, open to new ideas	Excited, optimistic
60	Organized, orderly	Courage, self-empowered
55	Obsessed, dependent	Low self-esteem
50	Superior, selfish, greedy	Jealous, insecure
45	Attacked, misunderstood	Angry, hurt
40	Failing, unworthy	Confused, indecisive
35	Rejected, isolated	Sad, lonely
Ultra-Low to Very Low **Energy is stuck and non-constructive**	**I think I am....** **I focus on all that is wrong and scary.**	**I feel....** **I don't understand emotions and they are toxic.**
30	Threatened, in danger	Afraid, frozen, pessimistic
25	Judged, demeaned	Hate, distrust
20	Treated unfairly, unjustly	Out of control, aggressive
15	Lacking morals, doing wrong actions	Embarrassed, shame, guilt
10	Unable to escape, no one cares	Hopeless, helpless, despair

Joyful tweeted, "That makes it all much easier to understand. But when something bad happens, and you get stuck in low energy, how can you change it to high energy?"

"That's a great question," answered Father Kindheart. "It's easy as one, two, three:

FORMULA FOR UPGRADING ENERGY VIBRATIONS

1. IT'S ONLY A THOUGHT, AND A THOUGHT CAN BE CHANGED
2. POSITIVE THOUGHTS CREATE POSITIVE EMOTIONS
3. POSITIVE EMOTIONS CREATE HAPPY RELATIONSHIPS

Joyful twirled in the air and said, "Okay, I get it. The colors change when energy vibrations change. Colors are pale and greyish when energy is negative and become bright and beautiful when the energy vibrates in higher frequencies." She buzzed with happiness. "So, when my electrical energy is vibrating ultra-high, it's easier to go super long distances during migration or to easily fly away from low-vibrating creatures... Or I could sprinkle them with jewel dust." She giggled.

Father Kindheart nodded. "Yes, yes, you have blossomed just like the flowers we love.

No matter what life gives you, whether it is good or bad, what really matters is what you do with it. Remember, you are a wise transformer, and meant to be joyful and free.

Kindheart extended his wings toward Joyful's face, and in a flash, he was gone..

Joyful was glowing as she felt rich with hummingbird wisdom. Looking at the garden below, she spotted her new friend Rascal Lee. He must've been feeling good vibes, because he was rolling back and forth on a carpet of purple flowers. He looked up and noticed Joyful watching him. He quickly grabbed a bunch of petals, ran up the tree, and threw them at her.

"Why did you do that?" chirped Joyful.

Rascal Lee smiled, showing his crooked teeth, and said, "Because I think you're magnificent. You see, before you sprinkled me with jewel dust at Lupee's pond, I used to hate everybody. I didn't care if I hurt someone or destroyed the things around me. I was unhappy. I felt alone, confused, and frustrated. I didn't know how to find food without stealing or hurting someone else."

Joyful noticed that there was a lovely golden color shining from him. She moved closer to him and tweeted, "Aww, thank you, Rascal Lee. Lupee did not like you going after her babies. And you did hurt one of them."

"I know, and I'm sorry about that," he grumbled. "I've been trying to make it up to them. I recently gathered bread crumbs and sprinkled them into the pond. They seem to like me better now."

"So, what do you do now when you're hungry?" chirped Joyful.

"I just eat those delicious apples, plumpy-bumpy berries, corn, seeds, or whatever grows from the earth," Rascal Lee reported cheerfully.

"But where do you find all those things?" tweeted Joyful.

"Well, I've made lots of friends, and we help each other. The squirrels bring me acorns. The birds drop berries for me. The ants bring me mint leaves. The trees and bushes give me lots of fruit and nuts."

Joyful smiled. "But all those animals used to be scared of you. Why do they help you now?"

"Because I've decided to become a guardian of the Garden of Great Love. I protect the birds by stopping thieves from stealing their eggs. I help the squirrels find new places to hide their nuts and seeds. I work with the bunnies by digging out holes and making them new homes that are safer. It's a win-win friendship. They're happy, and I am happy. And it's because you helped me see things differently. I threw flower petals at you because you are beautiful, my friend!"

"Ah, that's amazing," chirped Joyful, her eyes shining brightly.

Like best friends, Joyful and Rascal Lee settled in for the evening. Together they watched the sky turn from bright scarlet to a dark-blue canopy filled with glistening stars.

And then Joyful grew blue feathers on her neck, just like Father Kindheart.

Hummingbird Wisdom: Within a tiny seed is the power to create a giant tree.

CHAPTER 3 – BABY BLUEY FINDS HIS PURPOSE

The sun was high in the sky. Nearby, a young bluebird sat in the middle of orange hibiscus flowers. He was handsome but nervous. His feathers were bright blue, with an orange chest and dark velvety wings. Bluebirds are usually happy, but this one was not.

Joyful flew over to Baby Bluey. "Hey there, friend! How are you?"

Baby Bluey stuttered, "I . . . I . . . I'm okay."

"I feel like something bad happened to you, because you look sad and very tired," Joyful chirped softly.

"It's t-t-true something b-bad did happen. My sister was taken by a brown-and-yellow spotted snake, Mr. Dos Yardas. He was so, so, so big, with a l-l-long body and an ugly, slithery tongue. He grabbed and slurped my sister down his throat. In an instant she disappeared into his m-m-mouth. I was so scared, I didn't know what to do, so I flew. And then I felt terrible that I left her. I miss her so much, and I cry a lot," whimpered Baby Bluey.

"I think I can help you," chirped Joyful. "But first let me tell you a story."

"Oh . . . okay," said Baby Bluey.

"One day, a beautiful cat came into the garden. He was a very cool cat with a swift, undulating walk. He was called Mr. Slick. He seemed fascinated with me. I could read his thoughts like pictures that passed in my mind. He was curious about my flying. Maybe even jealous? It felt like he wanted to touch and feel my feathers. Maybe play with me? As I flew from flower to flower, his steely green eyes followed me. My instincts told me he was planning to grab me, because I saw his energy vibration become dense and dark. His eyes turned from a pleasant green to dull grey. Suddenly, he was desperately trying to catch me, flicking his claws right and left. He was unstoppable. His emotions were out of control, and his rhythm became chaotic. I was in danger. I zipped quickly to a safe place."

"I don't understand how you were able to see his energy change," squeaked Baby Bluey.

"You can't always trust what you see by looking through your regular eyes. It's better to see it with your inner vision that senses energy vibration and knows what's the right thing to do," said Joyful. When someone loses control of their emotions, they lose control of their actions," chirruped Joyful.

"But what about Dos Yardas?" whimpered Baby Bluey. "He was invisible as he moved up the tree, and he didn't make a sound."

"Yes, you are right," said Joyful. "Certain creatures are sneaky. They trick you by hiding their plans to hurt you. That's how they fool you. It's up to the wise ones to know the difference and survive. For example, if you sense low and high vibrations clearly, you can feel what's behind you and know if it's bad or good. If you can raise your vibration and do this, you can easily avoid the danger. If you're in high vibrations it means you can react much faster than one in low vibrations. Look at the snake who is dense and slithers along the earth while you are light and rise high into the sky with speed."

Baby Bluey whined, "I-I-I don't feel happy anymore, since my sister was killed by Dos Yardas. Are all big creatures of low vibrations and cruel?"

"Well, no," said Joyful. "There are big creatures that are kind. Their minds and hearts act as one. Like a dog who decides to nurse abandoned kittens even though cats and dogs are often enemies."

Baby Bluey's eyes got bigger. "Oh, that sounds nice. I've had a foggy mind since my sister died. I-I-I feel a big pain in my heart, and I'm always scared."

Joyful extended her wing out to Baby Bluey's shoulder. "It's important to know how to prevent the danger before it happens."

Baby Bluey's beak lowered, and he shrugged his wings and mumbled, "But I don't know how to stand up for myself."

Joyful continued, "If you want to be courageous, but don't think you are, first you must change that thought! Stop the thought, 'I don't know how to stand up for myself.' Instead think, 'I can learn new ways to stand up for myself.' At first you may have to convince yourself by saying things like, 'Fear does not control me. I control fear.' Repeat it until you believe it and then courage can be more powerful than fear."

Baby Bluey repeated, "Fear does not control me. I control fear." After a few tries, he looked less sad and chirped with confidence, "That does feel better than telling myself 'I'm afraid' so often. I do want to build courage, so I can outsmart snakes or anything else."

"Yes, when you truly want something, you keep practicing the new way of thinking and you will feel better, then your body will be stronger. Courage is going beyond your own limitation and creating what you really want. Would you like to know more?"

"Yes, that would be terrific," peeped Baby Bluey.

Joyful chirped, "Okay, study one step at a time. Never give up. Practice changing one negative situation into one positive situation. The more you practice, the easier and more confident you'll become. Practice, practice, practice can make you into an expert transformer."

Baby Bluey looked puzzled. "What's an expert transformer?"

Joyful's silky feathers softened as she felt his innocence. "An expert transformer can change negatives into positives and find positives in any situation. Transformers focus on finding solutions; they see problems as opportunities and find important lessons behind each situation. That way they are always growing, learning, and thriving. In this way you become wiser and can use your high electrical energy to produce a brilliant mind that rises above daily difficulties."

Baby Bluey fluttered his wings and sang. "That sounds perfect. I think my wishes are going to come true. I want that."

"I feel that you're still sad about losing your sister," whispered Joyful. "Tell me, if your sister could speak to you now, what would she say?"

Baby Bluey lifted his head and chimed sweetly, "She would want me to be safe and happy."

"Yes, I believe that is true," said Joyful. "Are you ready to learn how to become an expert transformer?"

"P-p-please. When can we start?"

"How about right now?" chirped Joyful.

Baby Bluey nodded yes.

Joyful continued. "I will send you mental pictures with different lessons. All you need to do is close your eyes and let your imagination be playful and creative. Here goes—from my mind to yours."

Baby Bluey closed his eyes. He was excited about learning to be courageous.

After some time had passed, Baby Bluey sang, "That's amazing. My vision became really clear, and I could sense different creatures moving about in the garden. Their energy would change! Sometimes it was hard and sometimes soft. Sometimes it had dull colors and sometimes bright colors. I could feel what they were planning. If the intention toward me was good, the color was pleasant, and the energy was light and felt good. If the intention toward me was bad, then the color was dull, heavy, and didn't feel good. Sort of the way you described Mr. Slick's change of energy from light and playful to hard and mean, and how his eyes went from bright, light colors to a dull, dark color."

"That's wonderful, Bluey. You're getting it. Are you ready for another lesson?" asked Joyful.

"Yes, yes, yes!" Bluey bounced up and down.

"Here goes," cheered Joyful. "I will send you more images, so you can use your imagination to delete what you don't want and bring in what you truly want. Scary things are made scarier when you are not in charge of your thoughts. Especially when you repeat the negative ones, because the more you repeat negative thoughts, the lower your energy goes and the harder things get. Then it's easy to get fooled about what's real and not real. Remember to stay present in what's happening now. It is only what's happening now that is true and real. The past doesn't exist anymore, and the future doesn't exist yet. What's most important is what you do now. If you're always doing the right stuff in the present time, then the future has great promise. And in this moment, you are awesome. You are learning to oversee your mind and wisely direct your energy," tweeted Joyful.

Bluey closed his eyes, and a few minutes later opened them. "Yikes, oh my, my goodness! I saw a scary movie appear in my mind. But I said 'delete,' and it went away. I am in charge. I can make those scary thoughts disappear, so I can feel sure of myself. In my mind I imagined that I shrunk the snake, and it became a worm that squirmed into its hole. Because I was flying far above, it really did look small, so I felt untouchable. I see that there are so many clever ways to use my imagination to change things for the better. I get it—I want to be alert, cautious, but not controlled by fear. I control fear, fear does not control me. When I am positive, solutions happen, and I feel fantastic."

"That's it! I knew you would be good at this," twittered Joyful.

Bluey fluffed out his feathers. He started to sing a song:

"I get it!

Create the life you want.

Unfold your inner wisdom.

Spread your happy seeds.

Live the stories you want to tell."

Joyful whistled with delight. "That's quite a tune you're peeping Baby Bluey!"

Baby Bluey was jazzed as he flapped his wings.

And then Joyful's cheek changed into an orange coral color just like Baby Bluey's chest feathers.

Hummingbird Wisdom: Imagination first and then you can make it happen.

CHAPTER 4 – MOTHER NATURE'S RHYTHMS

Joyful felt comforted, knowing that she had found answers to so many questions and had helped so many friends. Rascal Lee had become kind and caring. Baby Bluey had become smarter and braver. Joyful's eyes became brighter as love kept blossoming in her heart.

Surrounded by roses, she noticed her mother gazing at her lovingly. Karuna's crimson red feathers were shimmering with light. As they found each other eyes, Karuna's wings made infinity signs, as she sang Joyful's favorite baby song:

"Tweet, tweet we, Tweet, tweet be, Tweet, tweet see.

The seer is in you, the seer is in me."

Karuna was cherished in many gardens for her great compassion. Many birds and animals who had missing wings or broken legs, or had gone blind, had gotten better under her care and were able to return to their homes. Today she came to visit her daughter.

Karuna trilled melodiously, "I have heard many wonderful stories about how you turned enemies into friends and the weak into the strong. You are living the dream I always wished for you. I am proud of you. You remind me so much of your Grandma Treasure Full and her magical ways."

"These are the things you taught me, Mama. I am grateful and happy you are happy," tweeted Joyful.

Karuna's majestic crimson feathers fluffed up as her eyes twinkled. "I've come to remind you to never forget Mother Nature's rhythms. Knowing how to dance in and out of the five rhythms brings great freedom. I will send a picture of Mother's Nature's five rhythms from my mind to yours."

MOTHER NATURE'S FIVE RHYTHMS

"I get it, Mama," buzzed Joyful. "I especially love the stillness rhythm, as it connects me to Mother Nature and comforts me. I find the stillness rhythm in sleep, a power nap, in Torpor, or in just being in nature's silence. In Torpor, I am awake and aware of what's going on around me, and at the same time, I get a super energy charge. It's like how bears get recharged in hibernation, isn't it?"

"Yes, in the stillness rhythm wondrous things happen," Karuna said softly. "Like a seed that has a quiet calm inside yet grows into a giant tree that gives an abundance of flowers and fruit. In the same way, you came from a seed and have grown into a loving and kind hummingbird. When you close your eyes and connect with this quiet stillness inside, you recharge your body. The stillness rhythm is the one that all other rhythms come from and return to. In this peaceful stillness, we unfold our hidden intelligence and creative power. It is like how our garden's gorgeous flowers unfold and blossom every day."

"And the second rhythm is the flowing rhythm," Joyful said as she moved her wings with fluidity.

"You got it," rejoiced Karuna. "The second rhythm is seen flowing in rivers, winds, water and inside of plants and trees as sap. When you flow with life, you feel a grace going in and out of whatever you do."

"The third rhythm is playful, spontaneous, colorful, and musical. Like a kitten unwinding a ball of yarn or a squirrel jumping from tree to tree, it's all about having fun. Use this rhythm to be free and ever deepen your wisdom.

"And remember the fourth rhythm when you have important goals. The mechanical rhythm is steady, consistent, and automated like how the ants line up and march as they build underground colonies. Mother Nature is orderly and teaches us great organizing power so we may swiftly accomplish our goals.

"Lastly, the fifth is the chaotic rhythm. It can be wild, random, unpredictable and out of control. It can destroy or pull things apart like you see in fires, earthquakes and floods. Use rhythms of chaos to shake off what's not yours, like the things that you can't control. Then using all your other rhythms, rebuild something new. It will be greater than you could've imagined."

Joyful quickly demonstrated the five rhythms in the air to show she understood them. "I will remember to look for the rhythms both inside and outside."

"Excellent!" chimed Karuna. "When you understand how all the rhythms work, you can fly, play, and dance with nature wherever you are. Everything falls into its perfect place. And because you are connected to Mother Nature, you can migrate five thousand miles across oceans to get away from the dangers of cold winters. When in tune with nature, the wind gets behind you and flying is easy. When you want something sweet, flower petals will unfold and give you delicious juices that strengthen you. And when you are ready for the right mate, he'll show up in your garden at just the right time."

Joyful became very quiet and remembered Kindheart's words: "When the pond is perfectly still, everything inside can be seen clearly." In Torpor the heartbeat slows down from five hundred beats per minute to fifty beats per minute. As the breath follows the heart and slows down, a deep relaxation and renewal of vital energy fills the body. It's brilliant how a perfectly still mind can see things perfectly clear.

"Mama, I'm thinking of papa and want to send you a special picture I gave him."

Flow tree sap flow. Sap is in the roots. Sap is in the burly trunk. Sap is in the twisty branches. Sap is in the green leaves. Sap is in the flowers. Sap is in the sweet fruit. Sap is in me. Sap is in you. Flow river of sap, flow.

"That is beautiful," Karuna chirped melodiously. "But what does that mean to you?"

"It's the same sap in every part of the tree," Joyful explained. "Every part of the tree is connected by the same sap. And they are all in harmony. The brown branches would never say, 'I don't like your green leaves.' The flowers would never say to the tree roots, 'I'm pretty and you're not,' or 'I'm more important than you.' Mother Nature flows through the sap and loves them all the same. Each part, though very different, is united by the sap."

Karuna smiled with wonder. "Yes, Mother Nature gives the same love to each of us. She also gives us the free will to choose how to use our gifts. Mother Nature is rich, for the more love you give, the richer you become with happiness." As Karuna hovered above Joyful she sang, "This is who you truly are. A river of joy, flowing in and out of the Garden of Great Love. You are a gift to many, and many are a gift to you."

In a playful rhythm, they wiggled their tail feathers and made infinity signs with their wings as they hovered and pecked a kiss goodbye.

And then it happened: Joyful's neckline turned crimson red, just like Mama Karuna's.

Hummingbird Wisdom: From one cosmic hum all rhythms come out to play.

CHAPTER 5 – A CREEPY-CRAWLER TRANSFORMS

Later that day, Joyful rested amid colorful petunias. Across the way she noticed something moving vigorously. A strange object was hanging upside down; it seemed to be struggling and expressing chaotic rhythms.

Oh, I see, she thought. *It's a caterpillar inside a chrysalis . . . a see-through cocoon. Why, it's changing into a butterfly! There's a whole lot of shaking, rocking, and rolling going on. And listen to those squeaky sounds and quirky burps. I didn't know they did that. All this time I thought that caterpillars were sad, and that's what made them lock themselves up in darkness. This energy is dynamic—I see sparks of swirling lights. It almost seems like a celebration. That's extraordinary! I get it. That's how caterpillars transform into gorgeous butterflies. I wonder if it's going to be a monarch or perhaps a painted lady butterfly.*

Patiently, the young butterfly crept out of its chrysalis. Her silky wings swirled with dazzling designs of mauve, fuchsia, pink, and blue. The veins on the wings jetted outward, creating geometric shapes. Then as if on a gentle breeze, it floated over to greet Joyful.

"Welcome to the Garden of Great Love," whispered Joyful. "You look like an exquisite flower with wings. What kind of butterfly are you?"

"I'm a painted lady. My name is Flutterbye," she chimed.

"I am honored to meet you," chirped Joyful. "Please tell me—how did you change from a crawling insect to a buoyant butterfly?"

"Thank you, and of course I will tell you. I recognize you from when I use to crawl around this garden. You are Joyful Eve, the kind and helpful one."

Joyful nodded humbly.

"I started as a sixteen-legged caterpillar. I crawled and crawled from one leafy bush to another. It seemed to take me forever to get anywhere. I just walked and walked, chewed and chewed, and ate and ate lots of leaves. But no matter how much I ate, it was never enough. All I ever did was crawl and eat as the sun went up and down, day after day. Finally, I said to myself, I want to stop—this is humdrum madness. I don't want to do this anymore. There's got to be a better way. Then it came to me as clear as day. I'm going to change this creepy-crawler body into something that is light and beautiful. Because that's how I've always felt inside."

"That's awesome. I love it. Tell me more," tweeted Joyful.

"All right, I will try to explain," jingled Flutterbye. "Once I made up my mind, I found a safe place to rest. I used silk threads that came out of my mouth and spun a pad to hang from. Then I shed my skin one last time, which became a chrysalis. Alone in the chrysalis, it was completely dark, but I was not afraid. I could sense something wonderful was happening. All my body parts melted into a cosmic soup of nutrients, enzymes, and a brain. The enzymes dissolved my caterpillar body, and I understood how to make a bigger brain and transform into a butterfly. It's called *holometabolism*. The cosmic soup has baby cells that can create new animated life. All of this happens in about seven sunrises and seven sunsets. I felt totally in tune with Mother Nature, and I was determined to stay there until something amazing happened. My intention was clear: I was going to persist and persist until I transformed. There was a peaceful presence that was soooo comforting. I felt safe, protected, and guided by an all-loving presence."

"That's wonderful," sang Joyful. "You went from a sixteen-legged insect bound to slow crawling on the earth to an elegant, free-flying butterfly. Your insight is supremely wise. That's got to be the greatest accomplishment . . . metamorphosis."

"Thank you, kind friend," Flutterbye said sweetly. "I'm so glad you understand. It's fun to share this. I knew I was connected to something that loved me completely. Then I realized that once I came out into the world, I could pass on this great love by pollinating lots of flowers."

Then, Flutterbye sang a sweet tune. "When you give love, you grow in love. When love shines, happiness grows wherever you go."

"I felt tiny circles bubbling up inside me," said Flutterbye. "Then an awesome thing happened. I watched, as if above it all, and saw a little insect body that I once thought to be me. That's when I felt the tingling of wings moving and lifting. Gentle rhythms uncurled these brilliantly colored transparent wings. I was ready for flight."

"But didn't you struggle getting out of the chrysalis? Was the shell hard? How were you able to come out?" asked Joyful.

"Yes, the shell *was* hard," moaned Flutterbye. "It took the last three sunrises and sunsets for the chrysalis to soften. I used my sharp claws to open it and climbed out. I felt indescribably free. I am baffled to think that I once believed I was a creepy crawler insect but Mother Nature's plan is perfectly designed. Today I have wings to fly, float, and rest on pretty, precious flowers that will share their yummy sugary nectar."

"I saw your energy vibrating ultra-high. How did you do that?" asked Joyful.

Flutterbye gently rippled her silky wings wide open and smiled. "Yes, I would be delighted to show you. I will write it on my wings. As she spread her wings, Joyful saw all the awesome messages.

Joyful twittered, "Magnificent! You are a precious gift to the world."

Joyful was elated, learning about the gift of metamorphosis. As they were ready to leave the garden, she tweeted, "Thank you, Flutterbye. The Garden of Great Love welcomes you. Would you like to pollinate some gorgeous flowers and sip sweet, sugary juices together?"

Flutterbye lifted and jiggled her wings and said, "That sounds perfect."

Together they flew from honeysuckles to azaleas to hydrangeas. They sang the softest melodies. Their rhythms were happy, and their happiness was rhythmic.

And then Joyful's wings turned fuchsia pink and purple, just like the painted lady's wings.

Hummingbird Wisdom: Metamorphosis is the way to the sweetest freedom.

CHAPTER 6 – THE BLIND SPIDER SEES

It was a new day. There was a chorus of birds singing morning praises. The hills were celebrating. Giant trees gripped the earth with gnarly roots. Copious branches twisted and turned, reaching out toward the light. Precious life unfolded. Plants sprouted green gems. Budding flowers spoke of true love. The sun's warmth caressed all. Everywhere life was breathing in and out.

Every day Joyful basked in the scrumptious beauty of the garden. *I am wild about yummy sweets,* she thought gleefully. *Some flowers taste like honey, some taste sugary, and some like—wowie—heavenly ambrosia. Wherever I go I find delightful treats. Sipping, slurping, and drinking sweet nectar lifts my energy so high that I think that's why I can beat my wings twelve hundred times per minute.*

Even though Joyful weighed only as much as a penny, she could eat ten times her weight. Flowers vibrate subtle energy on ultra-high levels, and that's how they can produce such vitally nutritious juices. It was no secret that it was easy for Joyful to fall in love. Each day it was something new. The day before, she fell in love with the marching army of ants.

Joyful tweeted to the ants, "Lovely! Super job."

The day before that, it was the baby rabbits mischievously nibbling on their mother's ear.

Joyful peeped a piping tune to the rabbit family. "Happy hopping, honey bunnies."

And last week, during rain showers, the garden became so fragrant and fresh that Joyful lifted her head and sang to the sky with inspiring sounds of joy. "Thank you, life-giving rain clouds, the garden loves you, too."

Joyful spotted a bright-red rose near the waterfall. In a flash, she jetted in and out, savoring all the celestial flavors she could. As she looked down, she saw another hummingbird tied down on a spider's web.

She gasped. *I've got to free that bird before that hairbrained spider injects venom into it. I've seen that looney spider, Harry Bob, inject poison into his prey and do them in. I've freed many of them in the past, and I'm fed up with his nonsense.*

Harry Bob knew something had landed on his web, as it was shaking fiercely. He was excited that he had captured something big. He moved back just in case it was a danger to him. He waited for the creature to stop struggling. The energy and vibration told him it was a bird. With a snickering grin, he uncurled his pedipalps and licked them in preparation for his meal. His protruding fangs were sharp and ready to sting it with paralyzing poison.

Joyful zoomed in and landed in front of him. Quickly she used her beak and flipped him on his back. She was going to give Harry Bob a piece of her mind and teach him a lesson.

"Look here, Harry Bob," she scolded him. "You can't keep ensnaring birds and using them for food. I've seen birds caught in your web too many times. They jerk, kick, cry, and can't break free. I can hear their tiny cries echoing in the hills. And I've had to come free them each time. It's not right to cause pain and suffering. Don't you understand who they are and how they help you? They are the great pollinators of our garden. How do you think you're able to catch so many bugs? By destroying hummingbirds, you are really hurting yourself. In this Garden of Great Love, we have all agreed to DO NO HARM. We have found many nonviolent ways to survive and care for one another. Your wrong actions are not acceptable here. Either you change your ways, or you'll be forced to move elsewhere."

"Well, who told those birds to land on my web?" snapped Harry Bob. "You know I'm blind and can't see. How was I supposed to know they were great pollinators? My poisonous stinger is hard to control, and I can't help it if the web is sticky. But darn it, what you say makes sense. I don't want to move to another place that's filled with nasty critters. So, I apologize. Please go ahead and set the bird free. I really like it here and don't want to go through all the trouble of relocating."

"That's a wise choice Harry Bob. It's not just about you. You need to see the bigger picture inside your mind. It's about choosing what feels good for you and feels good for those around you. Even if you are blind, you can use your other senses to figure it out. Your heart has eyes too. If you sense with your heart, you will make better decisions and find that the Garden of Great Love will care for you too. I can send you an instant picture story to help you understand better. Would you like that?"

"Yes, because I just don't get it," snarled Harry Bob.

Joyful sent him the same pictures of high, positive energy and low, negative energies that her father Kindheart had previously sent her.

"Great jumpin' crickets," squeaked Harry Bob. "I get the bigger picture now. I want to learn the ways of DO NO HARM, and stay in the Garden of Great Love. It feels so good to be part of something bigger than myself. Something that is so stunning."

"We'll let go of past mistakes because you agree to change your ways for the better," tweeted Joyful. "Eventually these negative low-energy habits will dwindle and disappear. As your heart opens, your inner vision clears. Forgiveness is about letting go of past wrongdoings and committing to doing better from now on."

"Thank you, Joyful." Harry Bob smacked his mouth and grinned, and then he softened and glowed a little. "It's so kind of you to take the time to talk to me this way."

Chirping a fancy tune, Joyful smiled and knew things would turn out just fine. Then she quickly turned to the hummer that was tied down in the web and freed him. In an instant, both hummers shot up into the air and landed on the highest treetop.

And then it happened: Joyful's claws turned a shining black color—just like Harry Bob.

Hummingbird Wisdom: Turning trouble into peace lifts you up.

CHAPTER 7 – I FOUND MY MATE!

Joyful noticed that the emerald-green hummingbird's heart was pounding hard and heavy in his chest.

He looked at Joyful with disbelief and peeped, "I could have been killed! I don't understand how I could have let myself get trapped. If only I hadn't let my emotions control me and fear cloud my thinking, I could have escaped easily. That's never happened to me before. I'm sorry—I'm chirping and cheeping on and on. . . . Was it you who helped me?"

Joyful looked at the emerald-green bird whose iridescent feathers shimmered in the sun. He was very handsome, with a multitude of green jewels that danced in the light.

Her eyes softened and in loving kindness she chirped, "Yes, it was me. I'm glad you are all right! What is your name?"

"Delightful Hum," he said softly. He shook out his feathers as if to get rid of the bad feelings and moved in closer. "Thank you for saving me."

Joyful smiled, her eyes brightened. "I believe you would have done the same for me. Anyway, I'm happy to help. It must have been scary for you. I can see your heart beating fast . . . maybe you are still not feeling right?"

Delightful tweeted, "Yes, that's true."

"If you like, we can go into the quiet stillness of Torpor?" Joyful asked sweetly. "This always helps me to put things back together quickly."

"Of course," Delightful said. "Torpor is how I get my daily supercharge. After what just happened, it's a great idea to close my eyes, calm down, and restore my energy. Settling into quietness always clears away those bad experiences. That should do the trick."

"That's awesome," tweeted Joyful. "I love doing that every day, too."

They both closed their eyes. Their breath softened, their minds quieted down into stillness, their bodies relaxed, and their inner lights brightened. For Delightful, the stress of being trapped in the spider's web melted away. Joyful's face radiated with bliss.

After a few minutes, they opened their eyes. Joyful whispered, "Of all nature's gifts—beauty, rhythms, sweet nectar—going into Torpor is my favorite, because it gives me new joy and freedom, no matter where I am."

Delightful twittered, "Wowie, I agree. It's like having access to amazing treasures that are hidden inside. Not all birds or creatures understand the wonders that come from Torpor."

"I know what you mean," chirped Joyful. "It's like you connect with the main power source of nature. There are a lot of birds that think when you are just perching with your eyes closed, that you're being lazy, dull, or sleepy. But going to the source and getting a supercharge is the wisest way to accomplish more. Then it's easier to fly sixty miles an hour as we flash, zip, and disappear before the eyes of other creatures."

"Yes," chimed Delightful, "it's fun to watch all the garden animals and birds bedazzled as we zoom by, hover, and disappear. So, you must be the famous Joyful who protects the young ones in the Garden of Great Love?"

She nodded her head humbly.

They both felt happy perched side by side. Delightful had never felt such overwhelming feelings. He was convinced that Joyful was the one for him. So, he decided to do the "conquistador dance" to win her heart. In a playful rhythm, he began a dance, flicking and swinging his head side to side. He spiraled his wings as they flashed and sparkled in the sunlight. He was going to show off his athletic strength and wit. Joyful was mesmerized and watched his every move. Instantly he flew up a hundred feet toward the cerulean blue sky. Just as quickly he was zooming down right past her beak. And at the perfect moment, his tail fanned outward creating outrageous musical shrieks. Her beak opened, as if she was in awe of the spectacle. Then he repeated the whole athletic performance fourteen more times.

Joyful was not only impressed, she felt electrified. It was like being plugged into ultra-high electrical energy, and she was awestruck.

She thought, *Delightful is a handsome, bright, and witty hummer who's in great shape! I feel the playful rhythm chanting in my heart: Delightful Hum, Delightful Hum, Delightful Hum.*

Today, falling in love wasn't only easy for Joyful, it was awakening a part of her that had been asleep. She thought, *He must be my mate, specially sent to me by Mother Nature.*

As he finished his dance, Delightful perched next to Joyful and sat quietly, in peaceful contentment. After some time, he turned gently and said, "I heard about how you saved the koi family. It's remarkable how you did it. My garden friends and I enjoy telling the story of how you sprayed jewel dust and transformed Rascal Lee. I've heard he is now a wonderful rascal in the garden, playing tricks and helping many garden friends."

"Thank you. It's great that it turned out well," chimed Joyful, with twinkling eyes.

"Is it true that Rascal Lee teaches nonviolence to other garden predators who have the bad habits of doing harm?"

"Yes. He's a very helpful raccoon, that Rascal Lee. It's great having him as a friend and not as an enemy."

"And he's become a vegan?" Delightful shrieked with laughter.

She joined in as they laughed so hard, they both fell on their backs, kicking their feet into the air.

Joyful chirped, "Well, yes, he's vegan now. When your energy vibrates on a higher level, your mind and heart work together to act with kindness."

"That's astonishing," said Delightful. "And is it true you pick bugs out of his coat?"

"Well, I get a good snack out of it as well. So, it's a win-win," she chortled.

They both shrilled as they busted into gurgling laughter again.

"Well, we like helping each other," said Joyful. "Sometimes he brings me flowers with delicious nectar. . . . Oh, wait a minute, I know who you are. You're the one who wrote one of my favorite songs, 'The Message of True Love.'"

Delightful smiled and nodded yes.

"You're a chirping wiz, Mr. Hum," she tweeted. "That's some fine, feathered stuff! I often hear the butterflies sing it, and I like to sing it, too. It goes like this, does it not?

I know I am truly loved for I find sweetness every day.

I know I am truly loved for I live surrounded by beauty.

I know I am truly loved for many hearts send me love.

I know I am truly loved for I feel at home wherever I go.

I know I am truly loved for I live with a-bun-dance."

Joyful and Delightful chimed and chirruped. As they looked into each other's eyes, they knew. As their beaks touched, a promise of a lifelong partnership was shared. Instantly their wings revved up, beating twelve hundred times per minute. In unison they flew, swirling around each other while rising to the expansive sky. Below them, their garden friends jumped and cheered.

And then it happened: Some of Joyful's feathers changed to emerald green, just like Delightful's.

Hummingbird Wisdom: Even tiny hearts can feel love that is as big as the ocean.

CHAPTER 8 – TRANSFORMING TROUBLE INTO PEACE

Joyful knew it was time for their offspring's arrival. Delightful joined in and found the perfect tree—safe from wind and rain. He gathered animal hairs, leaves, twigs, and gooey stuff. In a matter of days, he put a nest together with his beak, feet, and wings using quick, mechanical rhythms. The nest sat tightly woven around a strong branch. For the final touch, he sprinkled perfumed rose petals and bits of eucalyptus leaves. The nest had all the right stuff. It was safe, fragrant, and comfy.

Joyful tipped her head side to side in amazement while watching from above. She hummed her favorite tune and swooped down to join him. They both knew there were two tiny eggs the size of rice grains growing inside her. When nightfall came, and the moon was waning in the night sky, Joyful started to have bad memories. She remembered how much danger she had seen in the garden. Her mind raced. She thought, *Bad things could also happen to my baby birds. Predators like Mr. Slick, Mr. Dos Yardas, or a different bandit raccoon could sneak in and climb up to my nesting tree.* She started to shiver as her distraught imagination took over her emotions. She pictured all sorts of bad creatures stealing the eggs or killing the baby hummers.

Delightful felt her energy vibration change and fall lower. He saw her cringe and tense up. He gently whispered, "I see something is not right. What is it?"

"I'm worried that our little ones will be in danger. I'm afraid of predators coming into the garden. They wouldn't be able to defend themselves," Joyful whimpered.

"Yes, that's possible, but we can prevent the danger before it happens. It's going to be all right," he affirmed.

Joyful snapped, "Do you remember when you were trapped in Harry Bob's web? It was your own fear that clouded your mind, and you forgot how to defend yourself. That's what is happening to me now, I feel I'm loosing control over my emotions, my body is starting to tense up and tremble."

Delightful shrugged and answered, "Yes, I remember having scary thoughts about being tortured by that spider. All those bad thoughts clouded my mind. I felt fear, regret and disgust, all at the same time. It was like a storm, and I couldn't think right. Yep, I remember, but that's in the past, and the past does not exist anymore. I have learned, and I'm now a smarter hummer. I am committed to turning any negative situations into positive ones. I am determined to have my mind work for me and not against me. By thinking good thoughts, I feel good; by focusing on solutions, I find answers to problems. By focusing on all the beauty around us, I keep my vibrations raised higher. Remember, Mother Nature supports us when we're connected with higher vibrations. Therefore, we are naturally guided and protected. By doing these things over and over, I have created a feedback loop that keeps my good feelings spiraling upward. There is no turning back to how I use to be. And we can stop you from going there."

"Thank you for being so kind to me," Joyful chimed. "I'm so happy to have you as a partner and life companion. You are rare among the male hummingbird species. Many of them just leave after they mate and don't care for their offspring. Then female hummers are left alone to care for the young. But with you it is different. I am truly grateful because you are so in tune with nature and your mind and heart work as one."

"I'm happy, too," said Delightful. "It's important to remember that we have a built-in switch that we can flip from down to up and on and off. . .. Hey, I have an idea for feeling more secure. What if we ask our friends to be our guardians? They can shield us until the new hummers learn to fly. Maybe the guardians can find extra food to feed those hungry animals. After all, most animals are content and won't do harm if they're not hungry or scared."

Joyful chirped, "Yes, I like those ideas. But I would also like to do one more thing to protect our future nestlings. I would like to visit my grandma, Treasure Full. She has great insight and is a wiz. With her guidance and support, I think my doubts will disappear."

"Where does she live?" Delightful asked.

"She lives in the east, on the other side of that big hill. It's called the Garden of Enchantments. Grandma is one of the wisest elders, and it seems no problem is ever too big for her. When I was just a wee bird, she came to visit me often. She taught me how to think with my heart and feel with my mind. Grandma planted the most beautiful, fragrant, and delicious flowers: white gardenias, purple roses, blue orchids, pink lilies, and yellow angel's trumpets. She taught me how to use the Jewel Duster to transform water into honey by using powerful visions, strong willpower, and a pure heart. Better to vibrate ultra-high, she would always sing. She would always tell me to stay in tune with Mother Nature and I would always be guided, loved and protected. I feel better just thinking about it."

"I would love to meet her," Delightful tweeted with a smile. Then he flipped his wing to touch her cheek. "You can count me in. She sounds astonishing. Let's go visit her."

Hummingbird Wisdom: The eyes of the heart see beauty everywhere.

CHAPTER 9 – THE GARDEN OF ENCHANTMENTS

After a short flight over the hill, they spotted Grandma Treasure Full bathing in the sun. The air was sweetened with the perfume of lavender and gardenias. The warm breezes carried fresh scents of eucalyptus. As she perched, her rainbow feathers framed her eyes, which sparkled like diamonds. Each feather told a story of the many wonders she had performed. The animal kingdom saw each color as a badge of honor.

Joyful sang as she approached her grandma:

"Hearts made of love, keep on blossoming.

Hearts giving love, keep on blossoming.

Hearts full of love, keep on blossoming."

Grandma Treasure Full chimed and hummed with joy, "You were a tiny hummer when I sang that to you. Mother Nature has planned it well because I was just thinking about you, and here you are. It seems that the kind winds have brought you both to me. I sense you bring me good news, and questions, too?"

Joyful embraced her grandma and nodded sweetly. "Grandma, it's wonderful to see you. And yes, there is someone special who wants to meet you. His name is Delightful Hum. He wrote 'The Message of Love,' a popular song in our garden. The news is that we've made a sacred promise to each other to be life companions and guide our young ones together."

Grandma Treasure Full hummed musically, expressing more than she could with words. Her relationship with Mother Nature was a very close one. Her peaceful, serene presence easily spread to those around her, filling them with a soothing calm. Throughout the years she had developed special powers. She knew, if you wanted wisdom to deepen and expand, then you must share your wisdom: teach it, dance it, and sing it.

The power of the elements of earth, fire, water, air, and ether were at her command. Grandma looked deeply into Delightful's dark-blue eyes, and chanted, "You are exquisite. You have dazzling rhythm. You hold great hope for our kingdom. I'm honored to know you are joining our family of hummingbird wisdom. Your offspring are going to be amazing hummers."

"Grandma," peeped Joyful, "we would like your guidance. We want to know the best ways to prevent danger and keep our nestlings safe. I'm worried, because during the past full moon cycle, predators have caused much trouble. Our eggs will soon be placed in our nest. Until the baby hummers become strong enough to fly, they will not be safe. I've used my skills to stop the danger before it happens, but what if I don't get there in time?"

Grandma Treasure Full said, "I see. It sounds like you are being controlled by fear and stuck in lower vibrational thinking and feeling. It appears you need to have a deeper connection with that permanent and immovable source within you. Then your instincts will be strong and there will be no doubts. You will know when to prevent danger and when you can just flow, knowing that nature is taking care of you. A heart that has united with Mother Nature lives without fear."

Joyful flapped her wings and embraced Grandma and chirped, "Oh, how could I get so lost again? I know the truth. It's true that my own insecurities have clouded my mind and caused me to be confused and doubt my own wisdom."

Grandma smiled. "Would you both like to come with me on an enchanted journey?"

They both tweeted yes at the same time.

With a sweeping lift, Grandma extended her wings super wide; instantly lights swirled out. Streams of multicolored laser lights shot out three hundred feet into the open, blue sky. In a flash the laser lights began to spiral outward forming brilliant strands of superior DNA in the sky. As Joyful and Delightful looked at the spectacle, their hearts flickered with excitement. A rumbling motion in the sky caused a huge boom and released the DNA that burst into shimmering specks of light, showering down like jewel dust. As the shimmering specks floated down and reached the two hummers, they felt the tiny particles of light enter their bodies.

That's when the magic began, and things changed quickly inside them. Their bodies' chemicals became electrically charged and pumped up with new, buoyant life. They felt like they were hovering inside themselves. Their minds were pulsating, and they knew it was metamorphosis happening. Their mental capacity expanded, and their minds were now able to access more intelligence. Their imaginations flashed amazing fun pictures of all kinds of possibilities for wonderful adventures and great achievements together.

Delightful's body chemistry changed and he became more luminous. Delightful noted that he was gaining new powerful tools. One of the tools he received was a "Mastermind Switch." With this tool, he could flip a mental switch and find dozens of solutions for every difficult problem. Actually, he didn't see them as problems—he saw them as challenges that gave him amazing opportunities to learn and develop super powers. He saw so many possibilities for fabulous, positive outcomes. It was obvious that his mind had been upgraded. Now it would be easier to care for his new family. Now he could dazzle, bewilder, or enlighten any creature.

Joyful's body displayed electrical sparks that flashed all around her. It was an auspicious day, and this was the best gift she ever received. She understood how Flutterbye metamorphosed. This day liberated her from any future worries. One of the new tools she found inside her was called the "Laser Beam Sweetener." It travels at superfast light speed and can stop threats and danger, or simply change pain to joy or fear to courage. Today she felt the rock of fearlessness inside her.

As Joyful looked into Delightful's eyes they both knew that Grandma's wisdom was planted in their hearts:

One: Connect with your inner source, in quiet stillness answers will come to you.

Two: Focus on building ultra-high vibrations to bounce back easier.

Three: See problems as challenges and challenges as opportunities for growing wiser."

In the Garden of Enchantments, Grandma sang a harmonious tune. "When you truly love without wanting anything in return, the secrets of the universe are revealed. Remember, no harm can come to you in the field of ultra-high vibrations. In love, the enemy becomes a friend."

Joyful and Delightful had visions of Mr. Slick, the grumpy, sad cat, getting adopted by Janet and Jack, the couple who lived on a hilltop near their garden. Delightful saw the couple's dog, Niki, run up to Mr. Slick with a welcome kiss right on the lips. Mr. Slick cringed but liked it.

With a silly grin, Joyful turned to Delightful and sang:

"A hummer hums a humming song,

And no one can hum the hummer's hum.

Unless you find the hummer's hum,

You won't be able to sing the hummer's song."

They both winked at each other and smiled. As they were about to leave, they noticed a gathering of garden friends. Grandma Treasure Full knew what was happening. At that moment, Flutterbye came swirling into the Garden of Enchantments with many other glamourous butterflies. They hummed endearing melodies. Many other garden friends came to see what was going on, and as they cheered, Grandma Treasure Full sang her farewell song:

"Your heart of hearts knows the freedom song.

Its lyrical melodies go beyond this world.

Simply love, without needing anything in return.

Dance with the great rhythms of life.

Enjoy Mother Nature 's treasures and don't

forget: A heart made of light cannot be broken.

A soul that knows how to fly cannot be caged.

It's the hummingbird's way!"

And then it happened: Joyful's tail feathers changed into rainbow colors, just like Grandma.

Hummingbird Wisdom: A soul that knows how to fly cannot be caged.

CHAPTER 10 – ENLIGHTENED BABY HUMMERS

When the hummingbird couple arrived home, their senses were sharper than ever before. Everything looked more alive, and the colors in the garden were glowing. Their vision could now zoom in like a microscope, and out for miles, like a telescope. Their Jewel Dusters created color combinations that danced like the northern lights. Their beaks became imbued with ultra-powerful chemistry that could neutralize poisons and mend broken bones. If they wanted to, they could create invisible walls to stop future predators from coming into the garden, though it is known that such creatures don't feel good being around higher vibrational beings, just as creatures that wallow in the mud do not like being amid flying birds. Using their imagination, they could project laser lights that could heal injured animals at a distance.

That night, Joyful laid her eggs. As the morning sun rose, two pearly white eggs the size of peanuts lay in the nest. Every thirty minutes, she turned the eggs to make sure they were kept warm on all sides.

Two weeks later, one of the shells cracked, and the first baby peeked out. She was featherless, covered in egg goo, and she wobbled around with a silly grin. The next little egg shook back and forth before the baby hummer pecked his way out.

With deep love for her baby hummers, Joyful thought, *I don't know where love begins and where it ends. How can my tiny heart feel this gigantic love?*

At that very moment, Delightful landed on the nest. He'd brought flowers with delicious nourishing nectar to share with the family.

"Right on time," whistled Joyful. The two baby birds opened their beaks wide as Delightful dripped bits of food into each one.

"I just had the most amazing vision of our baby girl's future," boasted Joyful. "She will be a tremendous transformer with pretty yellow, red, and blue feathers. Her name will be Serenity Star. I see her as a great awakener."

Delightful was buoyant as he flapped his wings and whistled, "I have seen our baby boy's future. He is sublime and has golden yellow plumage. In the vision that came to me, he is leading many creatures out of harm's way. He will be able to turn hostile relationships around into peaceful ones. His name will be Peaceful Hummer."

Three weeks later, the baby hummers were ready to leave their nest. This was their "independence day" to find their own adventures. Before flying off, Serenity Star and Peaceful Hummer had questions.

Serenity asked, "How can I maintain ultra-high vibrations when bad things happen around me?"

Joyful chanted with exuberance,

"It's as easy as one, two, three:

1. Focus on the positives.

Then watch wrong turn into right, hatred turn into love, anger turn into peace, sadness turn into happiness and fear turn into courage.

2. Seek and find.

The hidden truths, meaning of life, and lessons behind each challenge will be understood.

3. Act with compassion and kindness.

The heart will blossom new love and joy."

Peaceful waved his wings as he asked his father, "I know the real me and the false me. When I'm connected to the real me, I see the bigger picture of what's happening. I can hover above it all and respond wisely to each situation. But when natural disasters happen, I may lose myself and get clouded. How can I stay connected to my real self?"

Delightful responded, "Besides Torpor, you can stay connected to your real self by taking ten deep, slow and smooth breaths. This will calm, clear and brighten your mind. A calm mind will calm emotions. Calm emotions will calm your body. Then you will act wisely. If you get overwhelmed by the ever-changing ups and downs of natural life and react with unkindness to others, it's a sure sign you've lost your connection with the real you.

When you are connected with your inner source, you feel, see and sense the same unifying source present in all life forms. When you're connected to the real self, you react with loving kindness especially during natural disasters. Just honor and respect choices and differences in the animal kingdom. The proof that you are connected to your real self is when nature supports you in what you want to create. You feel uplifted and recharged every day. You explore and discover your hidden treasures and shine brightly."

The two young hummers were ready for new adventures and to say farewell, when they saw a large gathering below. All their family and friends from the Garden of Great Love had joined to celebrate their "independence day." They were so grateful for the loving kindness of Joyful and Delightful, that they'd brought gifts and special messages for their offspring, Serenity Star and Peaceful Hummer.

Lupee flicked her koi tail and sent the baby hummers a wave of grace. This gift would carry them with ease as they rode the wind currents to their new destinations.

Rascal Lee brought his partner and two babies. They created heart shapes with their long fingers as they beamed big smiles.

Baby Bluey circled around them, and with his imagination sprinkled bubbles of happiness that made popping sounds.

Mr. Dos Yardas, the snake, offered little bits of his snakeskin to keep them warm during cold nights.

Mr. Slick, the cat, meowed and meowed affectionately and swirled his fluffy tail in figure eights, sending them the message that infinite love will be their guide.

Fluffy Tail, the squirrel, brought his family, too. They brought tiny bags of seeds for the hummers to carry on their journey.

Thousands of ants marched up the many trees, making elegant decorations with cosmic designs.

Flutterbye and all her butterfly friends joined and created flowerlike bouquets that decorated the area with superb beauty.

The bunny family hopped over one another and shot grass confetti into the air.

Niki, the dog, howled and hit high notes that could reach the moon. It was an unforgettable moment.

Grandmother Karuna gave her grand-hummers invisible packets filled with ancient secrets to conquer the most challenging situations.

Grandfather Kindheart indicated to his grand-hummers where the hidden button was inside them, that when turned on would generate great electrical currents.

Great-Grandma Treasure Full puffed out two wands made of mystic herbs that could be used to make all their dreams come true.

The gnarly, twisty branches of the jacaranda tree showered them with purple flowers.

All the flowers in the garden were swaying, singing charming melodies as they sprayed the air with exhilarating fragrances.

The earth was breathing in and out radiant life in the joyous Garden of Great Love.

In a song of whistling shrills, Peaceful Hummer tuned in with everyone there. "I know that which lights the sun is the same light in you and me. I know that the trillions of sparkling stars in the night sky are also in you and me. From this day on, whenever the sun moves across the sky, I will remember that we are united by the same source. Thank you, garden family and friends, for making my light so much brighter. May the winds warm your back and carry you to the highest wonders. If you need me, just tweet, and I'll be there in a flash."

The sky changed colors as he sang his tune. The surrounding heavens were royal blue with splashes of violet. On the horizon, Mother Nature had painted the sky golden yellow and peachy orange with curly wisps of scarlet red.

In poetic lyrical rhythms, Serenity Star circled Peaceful Hummer, family, and friends. She was thrilled to hear his hummingbird wisdom and also wanted to share. She began to chant melodiously. "Dear brother, family, and friends, I know that which moves in the flower also moves in you and me. The sweetness that flows within the flower also flows in you and me. I know the humming melodies that come from the earth, stars, and moon are also inside you and me. I feel ever-new joy fluttering in my heart. I promise to uphold the constitution of the Garden of Great Love and all it stands for. May the hummer's hum guide you, to explore and discover the great treasures inside and outside." As she flew toward the east, she left a trail of shooting stars with a serene mist behind her.

Peaceful Hummer hummed with great calm as he stood still in a hover. In a flash, he shot into the sky and drew a huge peace sign that was a mile wide. As he flew away toward the west, swirling trails of dazzling light lingered.

The garden party of friends and family jumped, cheered, and whistled in celebration. Joyful and Delightful felt waves of bliss, which they expressed by fluffing and puffing their feathers. As their baby hummers flew away, they sang in harmony:

"Don't forget, darling ones,

A heart made of light cannot be broken.

A soul that knows how to fly cannot be caged."

Hummingbird Wisdom: Mother Nature's love can be found inside and outside.

About the Author

"Your presence is a breath of hope, wherever you might go with your message. We know the profound responsibility your work carries and the power your words hold."

—Los Angeles Educational Partnership

Acknowledging the need for literature that enlightens, uplifts, and empowers today's youth, Rosemary Watson was delighted to bring elements of her life's work together in writing this book. Gathering information and insight from her diverse experience in education, psychology, and spirituality, she was inspired to write *Hummingbird Wisdom for Kids*.

As an Adult School educator with the Los Angeles Unified School District (LAUSD), she helped over five thousand parents to improve their quality of life through healthy nutrition, discipline, play, and stress management. As a California Arts Council "Artist in Schools" multiple-year award recipient, she worked with over seven thousand elementary and middle school children. Her specialty, Creative Dance, focused on exploring and discovering new possibilities through divergent thinking, rhythms, and play. In her dedication to children's emotional wellness, she trained Adult Health Promoters to tour schools throughout the San Fernando Valley who would in turn train hundreds of parents in improving emotional wellness for their families. The program was funded by the Los Angeles Educational Partnership and Hathaway Family and Children Services. Prior to this, she was designated a "Governor of the Age of Enlightenment" by Maharishi Mahesh Yogi and taught meditation and yoga to the underserved in Los Angeles. She is a member of Yoga Alliance as an E-RYT 500 Yoga instructor.

Currently, she serves in private practice in Los Angeles, California, as a Ph.D. level, Licensed Marriage and Family Therapist. She has facilitated the recovery of hundreds of individuals from mental and emotional trauma, while helping them build on their strengths and restructure resiliency.

Rosemary lives with her husband, Murray, also a psychologist, on a serene hillside home surrounded by nature's beauty. Together they have been practicing Paramahansa Yogananda's Kriya Yoga for over twenty years. They enjoy nature's outings, biking, and camping with their community friends and animal companions.

www.ingramcontent.com/pod-product-compliance
Lightning Source LLC
Chambersburg PA
CBHW051349110526
44591CB00025B/2949